A Roomful of Flowers

By Paul Bott
Text by Barbara Plumb
Photographs by Kit Latham

Harry N. Abrams, Inc., Publishers, New York

A Roomful of Flowers

Editor: Ruth A. Peltason
Designer: Ana Rogers

PAGE 1: A generous bouquet of pepper berry, double pink lisianthus, pink phlox, 'Fire 'n' Ice' roses, 'Paso Doble' roses, 'Jacaranda' roses, hydrangea, ivy, and sweet peas in a cement urn provide a suitably dramatic foil for a rich silk damask table covering and basketful of variously colored antique yarn spindles. The rare bentwood umbrella stand deserves—and gets—a front-and-center position.

The photograph on page 108 by Lilo Raymond and the photograph on page 109 by J. Barry O'Rourke are reprinted by kind permission of the photographers.

Library of Congress Cataloging-in-Publication Data

Bott, Paul.
A roomful of flowers / by Paul Bott; text by Barbara Plumb;
photographs by Kit Latham.
p. cm.
ISBN 0-8109-3763-8
1. Flower arrangement in interior decoration.
2. Flower arrangement in interior decoration—Pictorial works.
I. Plumb, Barbara. II. Title.
SB449.B68 1992
747'.9—dc20 92-2690
CIP

Printed and bound in Japan

CAPTIONS FOR THE FOLLOWING PAGES:

LIVING ROOM: *The border on a log cabin quilt from Ohio, circa 1900, and the Stark needlepoint-style floral rug inspired the constellation of bright red flower arrangements. Amaryllis grows in a brass trough. White French vases on the mantel and piano are filled with hawthorn berries, hydrangea, trumpet lilies, amaryllis, gloriosa lilies, garden roses, and lisianthus. Arrayed in clear glass vases on the large, rustic Austrian cherry wood coffee table are anemones, dahlias, rococo tulips, and 'Estella Rynveld' tulips.*

DINING ROOM: *A beautiful formal bouquet in a white Limoges soup tureen is reflected in the polished granite dining room table. The stylish variety of stems—oncidium orchids, cattleya orchids, bittersweet, 'Jacaranda' roses, hydrangea, Japanese-lantern, and dahlias are kept low so as not to interfere with diners' sight lines.*

BREAKFAST ROOM: *This unusually spacious—and charming—breakfast room overlooks the garden, whence came the idea for the vivid green of the large Mexican floor tiles. A simple, old-fashioned arrangement of lavender phlox, purple dahlias, scabiosa, dill, and lisianthus makes a suitably informal counterpoint to the bentwood chairs and old barnwood table.*

KITCHEN: *This kitchen is so sunny, spacious, and airy that it could lure the most undomesticated of souls for cooking duty. Plants are dotted engagingly about the counter: two tall myrtle standards, two rose geraniums, and a topiary ring of serissa. Dill is used like a flower in both the pitcher on the counter and the bouquet on the table, along with lavender phlox, purple dahlias, scabiosa, lisianthus, and sweet peas.*

MASTER BEDROOM: *All-white flowers somehow seem the natural choice for this innocent and old-fashioned-looking bedroom with its antique iron-and-brass bed covered with two appealingly simple American quilts. Dahlias, lisianthus, stock, and Queen-Anne's-lace fill both a white crock and a white pitcher.*

BATHROOM: *A primitive piece of American tin folk art displayed on white wainscoting offers a cosy contrast to the marble sink top. The looseness and informality of a floor bouquet of hemlock, waxflower, stock, and scabiosa is echoed by a smaller arrangement beside the bathtub of white dahlias, stock, and lisianthus.*

CHILDREN'S BEDROOM: *When it comes to flowers in children's rooms, the secret is "Keep it simple." More obviously, perhaps, is the idea to make it fun and a learning experience. Here a beginner's array lines the windowsill—a pair of potted red kalanchoes attended by a small army of sprouting seeds, including tomato, carrots, and celosia, each in a pot with the seed packet as encouragement to budding gardeners. The twin iron headboards were made from the head and foot of an early-nineteenth-century French sleigh bed.*

Contents

To Curly, Es, and Bill W.

Acknowledgments

There are many people to whom I am very grateful. First I would like to thank Ruth Peltason, who is really responsible for getting this project on the road. Personal recognition goes to Rochelle Udell for a glimpse into what a book could be, and to Ana Rogers for actually taking it there. Shelly Latham and Kami Hawkins were indispensable at every turn, and I offer them my sincere thanks. I would like to thank Kit Latham for his patience and enthusiasm under the most incredible set of circumstances imaginable. Thank you Jim Weisse from Caribbean Cut Flowers, Dick and Rob Houtenbos, Peter Lozer, and Casper Trap from the Dutch Flowerline, and thank you Zaran Dunloy and Frank Cappola from Hawaiian Cut Flowers, who have been so supportive and who have provided me with the most beautiful flowers in the world. Thanks also to Terrence Koeniges, Dennis Kelly, Harry Sakell, and Tony Di Pace, who grow such beautiful flowering plants. I also wish to acknowledge Suzanne Maguire from the United States Tennis Association, Marion Davidson from Tiffany's, Bernadette Callery from the New York Botanical Garden, Tony Stanz, Barbara Lorber, Bruce Borderlon, Lucille and Bob Stortz, Bill Tansey, Stirling Zinsmeyer, Lois Heikila, Marilyn Bethany, Jordan Schapps, Marilyn Furman, Robert Greene, Tamara Schneider, and Lilo Raymond. For their fine taste and appealing wares, thanks go to Pierre Deux, Treasures and Trifles, Kelter-Malcé, Susan Parrish, and Cynthia Beneduce. A special thank you goes to Nancy Evans, Patsy Corbin, and Wendy Goidell.

The most important people to thank are my staff and friends here at Twigs. Without their willingness to accept more responsibility—and certainly without their complete understanding of this project—I would never have been able to accomplish a thing. They are: Louis Morhaim, Rick Meadows, Dominique Ho, John Wilson, Susan Montagna, Rita Sanders, Gary Re David, Debbie Snyder, Nicky Romano, and Dan Clancy. And finally, a special thank you to Mark Nobel Lockington, who gave a lot to me.

PAUL BOTT

A 1940s machine tapestry cloth, emblazoned with overscaled leaves in black and white, provides a stark and stunning backdrop for a late-nineteenth-century luminous blue glass vase overflowing with lisianthus, lilac, sweet pea, azalea, trumpet lily, bearded iris, and fritillaria.

Introduction

I did not grow up wanting to become a florist. In fact I had not even entertained the idea of opening up a flower shop until I was twenty-nine years old. Nor did I intend to write a book about flowers. Yet in the ten years since I opened my flower shop, Twigs, in New York, I find myself in the middle of a giant industry, writing a book about a point of view that does not generally bring to mind the term "florist" or, in fact, the idea of a floral industry. Rather what I do and how I do it is in direct conflict with what most of us think of as floral design.

I'm told that I break all the rules. What rules? Are there rules to follow for self-expression? Design is a sense. Design is a feeling. Design is an awareness of balance, of color, of romance, and above all of nature and ourselves. There can be no rules for good design because then the flower arrangements become too stiff, too studied. We need only to respond to our senses. Design is effortless.

This book will not teach you how to make a 3-tiered Biedermeier topiary, or explain any complicated techniques. Instead, *A Roomful of Flowers* is about having and enjoying flowers in your own home. I want to know how people live, who they are, how they think. That inspires me. So I decided to present a book that went room by room into the homes of many different kinds of people, and showed the ways in which it is possible to live easily and creatively with flowers.

My emotions are deeply tied to working with flowers, probably because I grew up loving them. I still have a vision in my mind of a time when I was very young and the world offered the greatest stimulation by way of my grandfather's garden. Curly, my grandfather, would bring me each day to what I remember as paradise—his garden. There I found comfort and peace. And I also found excitement: raspberries, rows of lettuce, mounds and mounds of blushing hydrangea. As I grew older, I joined my grandfather in saving other people's gardens. Curly would buy the rights to homes that had been condemned to make way for the rapidly growing California highway system. There we would head on the weekends, digging up abandoned gardens, saving the most precious plants and flowers from "progress." Such excitement! Imagine, it's just you, a shovel, and a garden, and a treasure hunt worthy of a chapter by Robert Louis Stevenson. The camellias that I dug up then are still blooming!

In some ways going to the wholesale flower market to shop for flowers is much the same as those days long ago with my grandfather. Such treasures to be found every day—flowers, hundreds of flowers, masses of them everywhere. For me there is simply no greater thrill.

This overwhelming experience is what got me into the business of flowers in the first place. I had moved to New York in 1980 to further my dance career. Dancers make very little money, so in order to make ends meet I took a job in that traditional fallback profession, bartending. As fate would have it, two of my "regulars" worked at one of the most progressive flower shops in the city. Over a period of several months we became friendly. One day they came in with a huge armful of flowers, saying that the shop had closed and that they had come to say good-bye and thank you. The flowers were for me. Straight from work to my kitchen at home, I carried my bundle of flowers, as excited as one could be. Slowly, bloom at a time, I began placing them in a large glass container, and just as slowly time came to a standstill—I was completely entranced. I was overcome with emotion and realized that I had to work and be with flowers on a daily basis. Within a week, I had landed my first account, and from then on began what has been a most satisfying, passionate, and sometimes tempestuous career.

A Roomful of Flowers is also about satisfaction and passion. My wish is to show how people enjoy their lives more by bringing the outdoors indoors. It is a healing experience to be sitting at a table sipping a cup of coffee and look up to take in some freshly picked flowers, or to wake up surrounded by tall spires of digitalis. Whatever the experience, it is unique, and it is ours to enjoy.

Although I love masses of flowers, I am fascinated by the personality of the individual blossom. Each one, regardless of species, has its own expression, its own way of developing and its own life span. Not every rose opens alike, and not every tulip will develop and mature in the same way. Flowers can be almost musical at times. As I watch them go through their cycle, sometimes I see a soft symphony of pretty shapes and textures and creamy colors, such as the gentle opening of pure white ranunculus or snowball hydrangea. Add to this 'Champagne' roses, pink camellias, 'Angelique' tulips, pale peach poppies, and you begin to take in a melody so easy on the eyes and so sweet to the senses that it is easy to see why flowers hold such beauty and mystery. For me, flowers sing with excitement and urgency as if to say "Look at me!" And so I do. I look for hours at the clever balance of their dance of life.

This, in essence, is what I mean when I say that design is effortless, and that in this effortless expression we are fortunate to be the eyes and the hands of nature in creating beautiful bouquets of flowers for our pleasure.

I hope that the pictures in the following pages will stimulate you to try new kinds of flowers or new arrangements; you may also find that some ideas are simply "not you." That's OK too, because it's important to feel comfortable and to find ways that please you to live with flowers. Remember that there are no rules; just give it your best. That's what I aim for each time I work with flowers. I will never forget the joy I first knew as a child working in my grandfather's garden, or the experience of making my first bouquet. I hope to bring that experience with me into every room that I fill with flowers.

PAUL BOTT
New York, New York

Good light and careful pruning keep this topiary conservatory in perfect shape year-round. On the floor, left to right, gardenias flank a conical ivy topiary, orange geranium, lemon geranium, wheatgrass, and rosemary; on the shelf are licorice geranium, curry, tall stands of myrtle topiary, thyme, a lavender topiary ring, and orgeano topiary. The herbs and scented plants are highlighted by framed 16th-century botanical prints.

The Living Room

*I*f there is one room in the house that could be considered ideal for flowers from a purely practical point of view, it would have to be the living room. Surfaces and pieces of furniture abound for displaying all manner of blooms, be they profuse, carefully arranged bouquets, or a single exquisite stem. And best of all, here is where the fireplace—the decorative focus of the room—resides. A mantel is as much fun for a flower fancier to play with as a canvas is for a painter. There is no end to the still lifes to be created with flowers, art, and favored objects. By changing the combinations, a completely different look can emerge seasonally or even day to night. Mirroring the wall above the mantel only adds to the possible permutations. The fire cavity itself can be enlivened with flowers or greens when the wood-burning season is over. A low coffee table or higher occasional tables provide homes for all kinds of arrangements, from baskets filled with small flowering plants to a crystal vase sprouting an orchid. The many lighting options in a living room—from a pin spot to pools of warm, rich light beneath a table lamp—heighten the effect of flowers.

It can be amusing to conduct one's own little before-and-after experiment with living rooms and flowers. For most people, looking at a living room after the flowers have been removed is a bit like drinking flat champagne. Flowers animate a room. They somehow give it synergy and make it glow. Even in rooms embellished with stunning collections of art and antiques, or yards of flower-printed fabric, nothing can compete with the freshness and joy of real flowers.

Usually the most important impression of a house is made in the living room, where tone and style are set. If clutter is the message, it usually shows up here first. And here is where we communicate a love of comfort or the pristine opposite: nothing is to be out of place. Art, objects, and books subliminally suggest a warm cultivated look. There are people who can read a living room like tea leaves. From it, they can tell you exactly what the owner is like, what are his tastes and ambitions. Living rooms set the pace of a home. They are the ideal setting in which to show off one's collections, reveal one's moods. They are the showplace of an interior, and as such are the perfect setting for flowers in their many incarnations.

One key function of the living room, of course, is to welcome visitors. Flowers make that welcome all the friendlier. They help both host and guest relax. They enhance the environment and add a spirit of comfort. Colorful and gay, they only evoke positive feelings. And they can be modulated to suit the occasion—be it a quiet tête-à-tête or a large, lively party. Spacious living areas actually seem a little lonely and sterile without flowers. A common denominator of life, they warm up a room instantly.

Balance is as essential to the placement of flowers in a living room as it is to the arrangement of furnishings. Variety is important, too—but within reason. Overkill in terms of too many flowers in too effusive bouquets can spoil the peacefulness. Often one kind of flower, like a bouquet of sweet peas with their jaunty naiveté, has more impact in a room than a voluminous, varied bouquet. A beautiful simple composition provides a breath of fresh air.

Art and flowers seem made for each other because of the natural chemistry between their respective colors and textures. Flowers mix well with other collections of objects, too—the vases and bowls one uses as decorative accessories double as fabulous containers for flowers.

Filling a living room with flowers celebrates an occasion and indicates to guests that this is a very special moment. But what a shame to limit the glory of flowers to visitors and festivities. What is important is to celebrate life with flowers on a daily basis.

Nothing feeds the spirit in quite the same way.

It should come as no surprise to learn that this plant-filled living room belongs to Paul Bott. Dominating the airy, white space is a glorious adonidia palm in a celadon Chinese cachepot. Two ivy conical topiary in garland pots and a black-olive topiary form the outer points of a triangle with the palm. Joyous spring yellow erupts in cut daffodils on a drawing table, wooden flats of tête-à-tête on a painted chest, and ranunculus on a green willow table. As if the flora quotient was not high enough, nineteenth-century botanicals were added to line the white walls. The chaise is covered with a green (appropriately) quilted blanket and a black-and-white striped throw.

A fluted Grecian urn filled with peonies, roses, delphinium, lisianthus, and chamomile becomes a playful counterpoint to the Edwardian column it rests on. Paul Bott purchased the Louis XIV chair, covered in celadon silk, from Gloria Swanson.

It's one thing to have a lucky find among someone else's castoffs, it's another to know a find when you see one. Paul Bott won on both counts with this eccentric, gracefully proportioned nightstand. Front and center, he positioned a classically shaped cream metal pitcher and filled it with a beautiful arrangement of parrot tulips and ranunculus. His wooden clogs reside cosily on the bottom shelf.

A wooden mantel, left natural, and plain walls give full play to the flair and simplicity of this still life. The busyness of the abundant flowers (zinnias, cosmos, Queen-Anne's-lace, marigolds, black-eyed Susans, sweet woodruff, clover, hosta, phlox, September weed, trumpet vine, and grass) is balanced by the exuberant hand-carved and painted Costa Rican fish. An inlaid box (50 cents at the flea market) and an 1820s drawing of Salem, Mass., by a twelve-year-old girl, balance the height of the flowers and fish.

This corner of Michael Quadland's living room is a composition in earth tones, whose sobriety is enlivened here by the floral profusion. Plumbago, delphinium, scabiosa, larkspur, stock, maidenhair fern, lisianthus, dahlias, and ranunculus cohabit in a glazed earthenware jug as comfortably as if they were still in the cutting garden. Even though this room is in New York City, shutters from the Mohonk Mt. House hotel (original paint and all) seem an appropriately countrified backdrop for a nineteenth-century American maple gateleg table, brass candlesticks, and glove form.

The graceful architectural details—windows, moldings, and mantel—added so much character here that Michael Quadland was encouraged to play down the furnishings. Two clocks from his extensive collection, an early-nineteenth-century grandfather from Connecticut and a Mission oak, function as sculpture. The colors in the flowers, which include 'Fire 'n' Ice' roses, dahlias, garden roses, and tulips, act as a bridge between a 1920s camelback sofa, with its original upholstery, and a Bessarabian flower-patterned rug, dating to the 1940s. The homey coffee table was made from a cut-down French pine table. If ever there was a rich, welcoming surface for celebratory flowers, it is this 1941 Steinway B piano. Hydrangeas, dahlias, roses, sedum, grass, and cut begonias work in concert to give a thrilling visual serenade.

Who could doubt from his living room that red is designer Nicholas Pentacost's favorite color? He strikes a bold rubicund chord with an elaborate gold-and-scarlet window treatment of his creation. The beat is picked up with an armful of ruby-colored flowers—'Bright Eyes' phlox, peonies, snapdragons, stock, and garden roses—tumbling out of a French glass vase from the 1930s. Boldly scaled flowers on the upholstered chairs incant a floral theme, regardless of the season. The French linen rug with diamonds and stylized floral wallpaper enhance the highly patterned room.

A glamorous piano, like this precious grand in high-gloss mahogany, doubles as an ideal display shelf for a bevy of flowers. The intense green of the celadon vases enhances the all-white arrangements of lilacs, lisianthus, and ranunculus. More white flowers—this time potted geraniums—are set near the windows, swathed in white-on-white striped muslin.

The medallion of an appropriately large and stunning Adam carpet inspired the color scheme for John Saladino's monumental living room. Twin sofas of his design are tall enough so as not to be dwarfed by a space that used to be a ballroom, measuring 23 by 35 feet with a 23-foot ceiling. Saladino wrings great textural variations out of the theme of gray: in the ribbed throws, the upholstery on the Saladino-designed chair, the linen cloth-covered table, the monochromatic painting, and the sleek gray metal chair. Pink highlights the room on a matching pair of seventeenth-century leather chairs and in the formally patterned silk and brocade pillows; a silver dish of clematis, coral bells, lisianthus, sweet peas, lady's-mantle, and peonies adds a perfect fillip of color. Tall 'Casa Blanca' lilies provide a royal complement to the splendor of the scale and the decoration.

The naiveté of lilies-of-the-valley in a beguilingly imperfect box helps to humanize the grandeur of the furniture and art in Robert Couturier's living room. The pure whiteness of the blooms is reiterated by an eighteenth-century signed marble cupid and a pair of Parianware statuettes. The cool architectural simplicity of a watercolor of a nineteenth-century ceiling is a refreshing contrast to the elaborately detailed Regency giltwood console and Louis XVI gilt bronze candlesticks.

What's appealing about placing flowers in front of a mirror is that the reflection provides double the pleasure, as in this rather formal arrangement of peonies, French roses, snapdragons, delphinium, campanula, and eremurus displayed in a chinoiserie bowl. Gold-reverse painting on a Regency mirror, circa 1820, is echoed by an eighteenth-century Swedish gilt-and-silver console. An English Gothic Revival chair gracefully completes the eclectic living room corner.

Flowers resting on the floor or atop a stack of books often seem more gardenlike than those sedately sitting on a table. Here is a case in point. Profusions of hybrid delphiniums, hydrangea, and ivy topiary surround a glamorous French giltwood chaise, circa 1880, like a colorfully dégagé floral wreath. Richness is everywhere in this living room by Robert Couturier: across the floor in an antique Aubusson rug and astride the windows in the palest of green silk taffeta draperies. Arrayed on a Louis XI table, stunning in its simplicity, are a nineteenth-century Swedish dish and a bronze statuette.

A cement garden urn seems an inspired choice for this gloriously colorful and generous bouquet of peonies and California garden roses. The choice of hues was inspired by the crimson velvet on a pair of Louis XVI gilt and green-painted chairs, a red antique braided silk coverlet on the wall, and the rug. In the corner a crisp pairing juxtaposes Arnold Newman's photograph, Igor Stravinsky, and a Charles X patinated bronze lamp.

This very graphic corner works well because the simplicity of the art contrasts so boldly with the ornateness of a carved Louis XVI console table with gilt on white. Bunches of sweet peas are (carefully) contained in a remarkable pair of fifth-century B.C. vases: an Attic black figure skyphos and an Attic red figure skyphos. A photograph by Robert Mapplethorpe, Thomas and Dovanna, overhangs the flowers. A Roman head of a young girl is marble; an Empire lamp, bisque porcelain.

A low-key flower arrangement of begonia leaves and dried grasses imaginatively captures the innocent spirit of the 1930s Beckmann painting of young boys diving. A collection of vases on a graceful English Regency bureau share a common medium—English marbleized ceramic of the nineteenth century. Of historic interest is a brass-handled heirloom box that was carried across the country in a covered wagon. The disarmingly simple, yet elegant, lamps were made from a pair of nineteenth-century French candlesticks.

The throwaway charm—and chutzpah—of juxtaposing a museum-quality Vuillard painting with Depression glass candlesticks shows the wit and imagination of Eve Stewart. A majolica pitcher, filled with sweet peas, dahlias, roses, and sweet woodruff, picks up the green of the painting, but even more intensely. Old lace, so intricate and elegant it becomes a work of art in itself, is draped casually across the mantel.

Opposite: *Two nineteenth-century Chinese porcelain vases echo the shapes and colors of the striking Italian still-life painting of food, also nineteenth century. An appropriately exotic choice of flowers—arachnis orchids, anemone, mini calla lilies, grass, begonia leaves, and 'Nicole' roses—captures the spirit of the eighteenth-century Italian console table and French painted wood bench. The unusual Austrian clock, circa 1800, is a European's fantasy of the American Indian.*

There's no mistaking Paul Bott's love of dogs from this living-room vignette in his New York apartment. He enthusiastically throws to the canines bouquets of 'Mister Lincoln' roses, 'Madame Georges Delbard' roses, and peonies for good measure—all in a Thai celadon glaze vase. To underscore the point, Bott adds an ingenuous nineteenth-century flower print of a wild rose. Vass, an English artist, created this oil painting of dogs in the nineteenth century; a century later, Bott's lively golden retrievers were cast in bronze and nickel.

Opposite: *A gracious arrangement of peonies, garden roses, delphinium, lilac, and foxglove in a Chinese cachepot looks of a period with the eighteenth-century Hudson Valley portrait of a small boy and his King Charles spaniel. Exceptional nineteenth-century Moroccan inlaid chairs flank a clean modern iron-and-glass table designed by Tom Penn.*

The color coordination of peonies, 'Jacaranda' roses, delphiniums, and lisianthus may not have been inspired by the painting of a nude by Van Jensen, a young American artist, but the hues and massing of the flowers certainly do balance it eloquently. Designer Tom Jayne cleverly utilized an old candle rack from a Catholic church as a foyer table and repository for part of his extensive art-book collection. The ceramic jars flanking the table and patterned bowl are nineteenth-century Persian.

Lavish bouquets of flowers in a Lalique glass vase and a crystal vase almost seem to glow against the dark walls. The purple tones of the stock, snapdragons, dahlias, sweet peas, and roses are richly appropriate for the brocade-covered sofa, velvet pillows, and collection of antiquities in silver and marble.

The indentation in the top of a splendid bouquet, composed of garden roses, foxglove, snowball hydrangea, sweet peas, lisianthus, and roses, completes a natural arc with the handle of a turn-of-the-century florist's basket. A small traveling mirror with a hand-tooled leather frame almost seems like an offspring of the grand leather-and-gold leaf mirror on the wall. A collection of patinated fruit by Jonathan Schwitzer complements the objects and flowers.

Simplicity itself—but what a powerful impact—is this still life of flora and blue vases on the mantel. The airiness of the flowers—delphiniums, lisianthus, French lavender—contrasts felicitously with the large, solid-looking, fluted Portuguese glass vase that holds them. A light blue sake jar is flanked by two ceramic vases by Becky Toderoff.

This living·room by Charlotte Moss is all about comfort, femininity, and elegance. Flowers are clearly in favor. Not only do they appear dried in a cement garden urn on the floor and rampant on the'table skirt and the chintz shades, but they are bunched in a delicate arrangement of fresh 'Champagne' roses, sweet peas, and garden roses in a Coalport vase. An eclectic grouping of objects precious to Moss are clustered on her table in front of a rendering of an Italian interior in watercolor. Lions are a repeating motif—in an Aubusson tapestry pillow and in statuettes on the table.

This mantel-scape is a study in reflections. A Venetian glass mirror sets the shimmering pace for a spectacular collection of nineteenth-century mercury glass vases and candlesticks. White ranunculus and paper-whites offer pure and pristine natural companions for silver and crystal.

Miniature Christmas wreaths of eucalyptus berries and 'Starina' roses look like halos on this charming pair of hand-tooled tin angels, who busy themselves as candle bearers. Spilling from the mantel is a wonderfully natural-looking assemblage of copper beech leaves, ivy, holly, hemlock, eucalyptus berries, and magnolia.

A fully restored seventy-five-year-old folding screen inspired the inventive tricolor window treatment. While the windows are fashionably dressed, they are not suffocated in cloth, so that precious sunlight penetrates to bathe the plants. The delicate fronds of a small platoon of ferns artfully balance the painted leaves on the screen. A pair of formal-looking trumpet lilies nod to a naive little bunch of wild flowers on the table.

A veritable trooping of plants and flowers gives a richness that seems in keeping with the silk brocade table skirt, silk-covered pillows, and graceful nineteenth-century painted screen. Setting off the screen is a terra-cotta urn filled with pheasant feathers, which almost look floral. They harmonize with snowball hydrangea, a pair of jaunty white hyacinths atop Venetian candlesticks, and a cement urn overflowing with variegated ivy. White anemones, shamrocks, lilies-of-the-valley, and an ivy ring encircle a botanical print. White potted cyclamen anchor the foreground.

Like a ferryboat floating on a sea of white, a sisal rug carries a pair of cotton duck-covered Bauhaus sofas that face each other over a wooden coffee table. Unbleached cotton duck curtains hang loosely at the windows. In addition to the work in progress, Robert Stortz's painting is inset into a white brick niche, which was formerly a window. Predictably, the flowers of choice are white—cut peonies in a glass cube and tall stems in slender glass vases. Other than the paintings, an Indian silk sari and Kilim-covered cushions heat up the room.

What better calling card for a decorative painter than his own living room loft. Here, Chuck Hettinger applies his skillful brush to a stereo set and backdrop wall that combine gold and aluminum leaf over a turquoise ground. Vibrant hybrid lilies project the sense of mystery and sophistication for the plenitude of dark-painted surfaces. Hettinger found the 1960s Venetian art glass vase—for a song, naturally—at a flea market in New York.

Opposite: Inventiveness, playfulness, and wit are surely the handmaidens of the design seen here. Imagination prompted turning this African zebra skin drum, circa 1950, into a striking table by way of adding a glass top. From detritus of the 1939 World's Fair comes this sui generis blue glass and stainless steel radio, surely a sculpture in itself. An exuberant bouquet of protea, cosmos, solidago, dahlias, roses, jasmine, and hydrangea pick up on the energy of the contemporary American vase.

The Dining Room

ining rooms present a wonderful opportunity for flowers. Here is where we enjoy delicious food, sense flavors and colors and textures. Here we sit down, relax, and open ourselves to interesting conversation. Here we gather in good fellowship with friends and family to indulge in the timeless rituals of breaking bread and sipping wine. The choice of flowers and the way they are arranged enhance these festive moments. Linen, china, and lighting work in concert with the flowers to give the maximum esthetic and sensual pleasure.

In many ways, the dining room presents the greatest challenge for creating a special atmosphere in a home. Unlike the living room or bedroom, the decorative elements are usually limited to a table, a sideboard, and a coterie of requisite accessories: tablecloth, napkins, glasses, flatware, and candles. Out of this *batterie de décoration*, one attempts to create a serendipitous ambience with flowers. It's a little like playing a symphony on a single violin or piano.

One of the first choices to make in decorating the dining room with flowers is what container to choose. Depending on the nature of the gathering, it could be a silver tureen, a family heirloom, a basket, or countless other holders—formal or informal. Ideally, the vase will not compete with the drama of the flowers. Crystal, uncolored metal, straw, wood, or stone afford the requisite passivity. A more flamboyant approach might be selecting the hue of a container to match the flowers, or other accessories or art in the room. Conservatively sized and classically shaped vases properly center the attention on the flowers.

At a formal lunch or dinner party, centerpieces, or table centers as the English call them, are traditional, but there's no reason flowers can't just as easily be placed on a sideboard or elsewhere, especially when an overflow of guests or an abundance of food suggest moving them. The recent fad of putting together table bouquets that are so tall that one has to look up at or sit under them now looks gimmicky. The trouble is that the focus of the entire room is on the overelaborate decoration rather than where it belongs — on the food and guests. The criteria that count when creating an arrangement are: Is it interesting? Is it beautiful? Are you choosing for just one special person or for a large gathering?

Since the table is the largest surface one has to decorate in a dining room, it rightfully gets the most attention. Color, texture, fabric all come into play. In a space with many small tables, different cloths at different tables provide a nice change of pace, as do quilts or silk textures or brocades. A table with all the reflections and richness of wood on display can look wonderful, as can the subtle marking of plain granite or marble tops. There is a similar opportunity for diversity in napkins, where color or pattern can modulate the tenor of the decor.

Flower colors are often selected to harmonize with the shade of the room and the table linen. The menu itself can also be a determining factor. Wild game with a cranberry chutney, for example, calls for flowers deep in hue, perhaps with burnt oranges and reds mixed in. An early summer salad might summon nasturtiums or sprays of pansies. Since sensuality is a key ingredient in the enjoyment of flowers, blooms with some fragrance, like lily-of-the-valley or jonquils, are obvious choices. The warmth of a candle-lit room, however, intensifies fragrances, so gardenias and paper-whites should be avoided because of their strong scent.

Some people prefer just one kind of flower; others, a mixture. With several round tables in the dining room, one lively possibility is to have roses on one table, tulips on another, ranunculus on a third. Guests, who tire of gazing at tables that are boringly the same, appreciate a little unpredictability. Another charming option might be nosegays or sweetly fragrant tussy mussies at each place. Guests enjoy taking them home when they leave the party.

No decoration is more appropriate in the dining room than candles. They are the requisite finishing touch, enhancing the appearance of the food and flowers, and adding an overall soothing ambience. Almost all candles—be they votive, tapers, fat beeswax, or hurricane lamps—mix well. Varying the shade of candles slightly from one surface to another—parchment to ivory, pale pink to flesh—provides a subtle variation on a theme.

In decorating the dining room with flowers, the important thing is to have fun expressing your individual style, be that old-fashioned or modern, ornate or simple. When arranging flowers, as when putting together the dinner party itself, what's important is creating an atmosphere where you and your guests—or even just you alone—will have a lovely time.

Chuck Hettinger managed to coax synergy out of his dining-room table by glueing a mahogany top onto an unrelated pedestal base and then painting the top in gold and composition leaf. Though no one else in his family wanted the 1950s turquoise leather dining chairs when they became available, Chuck immediately envisioned them around his table. How right he was. An original art print by Stanley Moss inspired the color choice of the dahlias and zinnias, clustered in the black-and-white vases. A pet fish, swimming across the bare floor, is Chinese Modern, vintage 1950.

Recognizing that a large, single-use, formal dining room is a bit of a rara avis in the 1990s, designer Charlotte Moss informalized hers ever so slightly with a sisal carpet. Flower arrangements on the large Regency dining table and the eighteenth-century English demi-lune side tables, composed as they are of hydrangea, lisianthus, stock, dahlias, and garden roses, look like they were spirited from an English country house. A late Regency breakfront houses a rather spectacular collection of English porcelain—Coalport, Spode, and Ridgeway. The magnificent crystal chandelier is eighteenth-century Russian.

What could be more appealing than breakfast just outside the bedroom? A cheerful arrangement of garden roses, blue hydrangea, jasmine, snow-on-the-mountain, and dahlias, arranged on a pink paisley throw, ushers in the day on a high note. A leather-trimmed quilted curtain behind the table slides to cover the bedroom doorway.

Purples and lavenders are suitable partners for the predominant grays and beiges of this banquette eating nook, which works for snacks, tea or coffee, or a quick breakfast. Campanula, thistle, tweedia, and lace flower have the spontaneity of wild stems plucked from a field or alongside the road.

A mélange of apricot, suede, pink, and 'Angelique' tulips in Italian pottery cachepots, vintage 1950s, helps to soften this very masculine, rather stark dining room with its collection of antlers and skulls. The food is sure to be varied, as there are more than 2,000 cookbooks to choose from on shelves running all around the room. Earthenware plates, antique silver cutlery, and hand-blown stemware, set directly on the seventeenth-century walnut library table, highlight the beauty of the wood.

Few would guess that this spacious, airy, country-looking kitchen, which gives onto a garden through French doors, is located in the heart of New York City. Lavender topiary in small terra-cotta pots complement the wispy array of flowers (serissa, plumbago, September aster, solidago, and cut strawberry vines), which is kept intentionally low-key so as not to compete with the rare and treasured view of the garden.

Wide-plank polished wood floors, ladderback chairs with rush seats, and a pine harvest table immediately suggest a country-style theme. A low, loose arrangement of cut amaryllis, begonias, dahlias, and hydrangea in a carved wooden American bowl repeat the autumnal colors of the Tiffany-style lamp shade, as do the miniature pumpkins.

A striking American quilt, vintage 1920, hung on the wall like the artwork it is, cues the provincial mood of the table and its accoutrements, a mix of fine antiques and flea-market finds. The pale colors of the flowers—double lisianthus, hydrangea, and cut begonia—play against the vivid hues of the quilt. Antique green Wedgwood plates, Roseville candlesticks, and a "graniteware" enamel pot, used as a vase, reinforce the informal mood.

This sunny corner provides an ideal venue for breakfast for two. There's no mistaking the owner's passion for twig furniture. The amazing bent willow bird cage, which is a real piece of architecture, was made by Tim Barber in Hane City, Florida. A summer arrangement of wild rambling roses, strawberry vines, and wild sweet pea spills buoyantly out of a pewter vase.

A flair for the dramatic has the upper hand here, both in the hand-painted screen and theatrical gold leaf chandelier with its dangling crystals. The flowers look positively prim in comparison—hydrangea, lisianthus, dahlias, and roses.

An unusual blending of sunflowers with gloriosa lilies, dahlias, snapdragons, butterfly weed, roses, stock, and astilbe virtually upstage everything else in the room. And that is no mean feat considering the beauty of the English Regency table, chairs, and sideboard. The blooms are so abundant that just the merest corner of a Chinese bowl peeks through. An ornate Regency convex mirror adds yet another layer of richness to the nineteenth-century scenic wallpaper mural.

If ever there was a table that celebrated the tender, first day of spring or May Day, this one by Paul Bott is it. Sitting around this table, or even just looking at it, how could anyone not feel sunny, happy, renewed? Woodland moss keys the verdant theme, taken up in turn by pots of lily-of-the-valley, green wine goblets, and a celadon brocade cloth. The delightfully eccentric painted bronze nineteenth-century candlesticks, dubbed "The Maidens," are in a race for most unusual with the nineteenth-century inlaid Moroccan teakwood chairs.

The Kitchen

*K*itchens, be they the no-nonsense high-tech variety or the countrified homey type, attract family and friends much like pollen-rich flowers do bees. Who can resist investigating what's for dinner, or checking up on seductive food smells that will soon appease gnawing appetites. Even more, it's fun to put your elbows on the counter, sip a glass of wine, and chat with the cook. "Hanging out" in the kitchen reinforces our best memories of childhood and other happy, convivial moments in our lives.

Flowers in the kitchen add one more sensual emollient to those already there in abundance, such as richly colored fruit and vegetables, ruddy terra-cotta casseroles, and burnished copper pots. A couple of roses in a carafe, some daisies in a drinking glass, or a squash blossom in a small bud vase provide the appropriate note of piquant casualness. They also give the cook something pretty to look at as he or she tends to the meal. Nothing overly fussy or too large. These encroach upon precious counter space and are vulnerable to being knocked over when food preparations or late-night cleanup gets frenzied. On the other hand, if take-out is your menu, it might be fun to fill some of your spare counter space with an imaginative three-dimensional botanical still life. In real working kitchens, though, any clutter, no matter how florally correct, impinges upon the important culinary work at hand.

Ideally, you would snip a few kitchen flowers in your own garden and bring them in. This makes more sense than spending money at a florist. When cooking is in full swing, kitchens get so hot that stems have a brief life at best.

Containers that seem most beguiling for blooms in the kitchen are the natural-looking, earthy ones, like terra-cotta pots, rustic baskets, or olive-wood bowls. A creamer or mug is appropriately down scale for a newly picked bouquet. Whatever is easy works best. Avoid having the flowers in your kitchen look as if you have lavished more attention on them than the food. Pots of flowers, lined up on a shelf in front of the kitchen window, make sense, too. They are less trouble than cut flowers and they last longer.

Many serious cooks banish flowers from the kitchen on principle because they feel they get in the way. They prefer their living nature to come from herbs—basil, tarragon, thyme, or even wheatgrass. To remain healthy, though, these herbs must bask in sunshine, and a window ledge or an adjacent shelf is a logical choice. If that's inconvenient, an attractive substitute would be a French aluminum stretch basket, which usually stores potatoes or onions. The three shelves can accommodate a pot or two of the herbs on each level.

The warmth and humidity of the kitchen makes it the ideal place for forcing bulbs in February. Tulips, amaryllis, paper-whites, and daffodils sprout quickly in a sunny window and become joyous harbingers of spring. African violets succeed brilliantly in the kitchen too, as does the faithful avocado seed suspended on toothpicks in a glass jar.

Occasionally a breakfast room adjoins the kitchen. There one can go all out for special occasions. A cobalt blue vase bristling with sunflowers cannot help but bring gaiety and energy to a Sunday afternoon brunch. And what could be simpler and more springlike than a big flat of red or yellow tulips on a late winter's day? A more offbeat idea would be to grow a head of lettuce in a clay pot. When it comes into full flower, it makes a charming and unusual centerpiece. The cook who does not have a marvelous view of the outdoors cherishes any small bit of nature growing, be it a single flower or an herb topiary.

Although this engagingly eclectic kitchen is a cook's dream in its step-saving compactness, it still has room for an appealing variety of floral bouquets. The foreground pitcher overflowing with dahlias is echoed by more dahlias in a pitcher on an Early American jelly cabinet. This go-round they are combined with sweet peas and 'Jacaranda' roses. An old-fashioned basket on a hickory bench, circa 1910, holds freshly cut dill, waxflowers, and roses. On the wall, a turn-of-the-century French railroad clock adds a bold graphic touch to a charming juxtaposition of a modern poster by Carol Anthony and a New Hampshire watercolor in its original frame dating from the 1850s.

STOP METRIC MADNESS

wine
cheese
flowers

One of the most important decorative elements in any kitchen also happens to be the most functional: the cabinet. Here an elegantly simple rosewood design with round metal pulls displays a handsome collection of Deruta pottery from Italy. Rustic tiles on the wall and backsplash key the warm, countrified feeling of the room. Flowers in abundance line the birch-trimmed stone divider counter. In succession: a tall, generous bouquet of stock, a compact array of Dutch tulips, and a tall assemblage of California garden roses. More roses and delicate peach parrot tulips flank the double sink.

What could be a more classic room for a still life than a kitchen? Painters have always found food and implements irresistible subject matter because of their basic simplicity, charm, texture, and color. The airy pairing of wild field grasses and pepper berry naturally synchronizes with the down-home assemblage of American spongeware, mid-nineteenth-century American crockery, French country egg basket, and contemporary birdhouse.

An American country hutch in hues of red and white provides the perfect backdrop—at once austere and warm—for an extensive collection of majolica. Though treasured, the pieces are at hand to be used and enjoyed. As a peaches-and-cream accent to the blues and greens of the pottery is the heaping bouquet of 'Apricot Beauty' tulips and 'Gerdo' roses.

A turned balustrade, found in the trash and left as was with its worn paint finish, gives a bit of architectural élan to a standard kitchen window. To stretch the storage space in this small apartment, German fruit plates and an antique pitcher and bowl are kept on the window shelf. A classic rounded terra-cotta vase holds a loose, light-hearted arrangement of mock orange, raspberry vines, wild phlox, chamomile, and buttercups.

Miniature potted azaleas, evocative of geraniums with all their charm but more unusual, make ideal kitchen plants—particularly if there is ample sunlight. The all-white room is enhanced by its more unusual attributes: a 1930s toaster that actually works, and a dissembler that is really a salt and pepper shaker. The whimsical Hershey's lighted display clock is a cherished flea-market find. Tulips and ranunculus add an explosion of color to the monochromatic color scheme.

Wooden beams, wood-paneled walls, and wooden cabinets set a cozy, welcoming atmosphere in this large and airy country kitchen with its lovely outdoor views. There's no mistaking the fact that this is a serious cook's kitchen from the shiny battery of hanging copper pots, the super-sized, well-worn chopping block in the foreground, and the restaurant stove against the wall. With such a generous amount of work space, there is always plenty of room for flowers from the cutting garden. Profiled gracefully against the window are a tall bunch of daylilies and a wispy ivy ring in a clay pot. A squash flower clipped in the vegetable garden sticks up jauntily from a glazed ceramic vase.

Anyone who loves food and is fascinated by its preparation and the accoutrements that go with it finds eat-in kitchens appealing. This one features a further amenity—a blissfully bucolic view. Two tables, one of which conveniently doubles as a preparation area, accommodate the hordes of hungry sociable people likely to congregate here. An antique rush armchair invites kibitzers to lend moral support to the cook. A garden off the kitchen offers the advantage of spontaneous floral arrangements, such as this charming blending of blooms—scabiosa, blue hydrangea, lady's-mantle, wild ferns, astilbe, and cut herbs.

French sunflowers seem the irresistibly obvious accompaniment to food that happily evokes the south of France or Italy, such as these ripe red tomatoes and vivid yellow, red, and green peppers. The smiley faces of the sunflowers invite sunny thoughts of wanderlust.

Aroma is kith and kin to the kitchen, and plants such as bulbs and herbs can only enhance the pleasure. The bunched paper-whites and garden-sized rosemary each perfume the air. Potted begonias, amaryllis, and the tête-à-têtes in the bean pot are a colorful foil to the cook's daily menu.

The Bedroom

*S*trange as it may seem, the Victorians believed that sleeping with flowers in the bedroom was unhealthy. So when they turned down the sheets at night, out went the blossoms. Happily for us, attitudes have shifted one hundred eighty degrees since then. Now one of our most blissful sensations can be opening our eyes in the morning, preferably with bird song in the background, and seeing the sun slanting in an open window and suffusing a single beautiful stem on our bedside table or a delicate bouq et on the dresser with gentle morning light.

When guests are coming to stay, one of the the first things we think of is placing welcoming flowers in their bedroom. Everyone responds gratefully to this considerate gesture of greeting. Bouquets do not have to be grandiose or extravagant to be adored. In fact, what is more charming than a few stems fresh from the garden in a pitcher or a single rose in a bud vase?

For most of us, the bedroom is where we spend much of our downtime relaxing. This is the room where we unwind, where we can be most ourselves. This is the room that is our haven for contemplating and for restoring our energy and drive to return to the fray yet another day. We spend a lot of regenerative time in the bedroom. Here we enjoy reading, relaxing, lounging, listening to music—perhaps even eating. Wherever living is going on with verve and pleasure, flowers have to be part of the process.

Since the bedroom is quintessentially a place of rest, designed to foster serenity, inner peace, ease, tranquillity, and calm, flower arrangements there should not be too complicated. They should not appear fussy. They should have what Paul Bott calls "significant simplicity." Even in very decorated bedrooms with lots of elements and many little treasures, he turns down the volume by choosing one kind of flower in one color. Wild flowers are particularly attractive for a bedroom because of their naiveté and simplicity. Even when no field or meadow is at hand to collect them from, it is often possible to discover them at a local farmer's market. One of Paul Bott's favorite flowers for the bedroom is Solomon's-seal, with its appealing pure green color. He particularly likes putting unpretentious cosmos near a bedroom window to catch the sunlight. Hydrangeas please both esthetically and practically. They are very soothing and last almost forever. Even though one may set one's heart on a favorite flower for the bedroom, such as cosmos, seasonality can thwart plans. In winter cosmos is nowhere to be found. Nor is Bott's favorite for his own bedroom—dahlias—available out of season. But quick modern transportation affords all year long the luxury of an attractive selection of flowers suited to the bedroom. Flowering plants also make nice additions, or even substitutes, because they last much longer than bouquets.

One of the most cherished characteristics of flowers—their heavenly natural fragrance at once sweet and sensual—seems especially well suited to the bedroom. One whiff of a bunch of lilacs can set you up for an entire day. Two flowers in Paul Bott's pantheon of bedroom preferences are lily-of-the-valley and lilac. Their fragrance is subtle, and even when older, they don't develop a rancid odor. With aroma in a bedroom, however, a little goes a long way.

The scent of lilies, for example, can be overpowering.

Color is yet another bounty of pleasure from flowers in the bedroom. An all-white room or a beige or a black-and-white one cries out for this spritz of visual excitement. Magentas, maroons, and hot pinks are particularly favored by Bott for their warmth and sophistication. When considering color, the choice of container is just as important; flower containers should echo the taste of the person who lives there. They might be as formal as a silver bowl or as simple as a glass cylinder, an earthenware pitcher, or a brass urn.

Flowers can be positioned just about anywhere in a bedroom, even right on the floor if the vase is large and steady. A low stool, if it is not upholstered, might hold a small bouquet, so might an antique box or a stack of books. In front of a mirror is a felicitous spot for flowers because one sees twice as many reflected.

No matter what the stylistic message of a bedroom, this is where we greet the day and bid farewell to the night. How sweet and refreshing to experience these timeless rituals of life with flowers as part of the mise-en-scène.

The charm of Paul Bott's bedroom derives from its exuberant energy and diversity of fascinating finds. Keenly enjoying the pleasure of seeing flowers first thing in the morning and last thing at night, Paul is lavish with them. He practically surrounds his wonderfully romantic iron bed with pots of pink foxglove, and a palm with a tracery of fronds that his ginger cat, Maisy, likes to chew. Even the chartreuse wall is plantlike, echoing as it does the color of lady's-mantle, the first green color of spring. Bursts of flowers race across a nineteenth-century painted leather screen and onto the 1950s cotton pillows.

The right flowers in the right scale and colors can turn even the blandest door of a bedroom into a focal point. This generous arrangement of lilac, lady's-mantle, Solomon's-seal, grass, and campanula in an oversized clear glass cube balanced on a small antique oak plant stand would demand attention, even without the straw hat. Lilacs bring the springlike theme into the room, with the impression that they were just brought in from the garden only moments ago. They are the perfect enhancements for this spartan bedroom. Decoration is provided by a collection of old English photographs and small Victorian lithographs.

Lacy yellow oncidium orchids complement this regal bedroom by French designer Robert Couturier. White cotton duck drapes the windows, floor to ceiling, making a surprising but inspired background for an imposing gold-edged border of maroon brocade, a luxurious French silk bedspread, and an eighteenth-century Indian rug embellished with gold embroidery. The tailored bed is a suitably quiet foil for the ornately framed, beautiful portrait of a young woman.

Talk about peace and serenity and getting as far away from stress as possible! This chaste bedroom suggests all those good things. White unbleached duck curtains close it off from the rest of the apartment, yet white painted floors give it continuity with the adjoining space. The only touch of hedonism is a gold-framed mirror. The two clear glass vases, holding lilacs in the foreground and Solomon's-seal at the head of the bed, seem appropriately uncomplicated.

Bare wood floors, white walls, and a sparely detailed mantel provide a neutral backdrop for the amusing pyrotechnics of geometric shapes—an assortment of weathervanes, a lightning rod, and a wind velocity and direction arrow. The curves of a framed old-fashioned window from Upstate New York contrast with the straight ribs of the brass bed and the skip squares of an old American quilt. The multiple eruptions of the hydrangeas pick up on and animate the room's playful details.

This joyful bedroom exemplifies the wit and whimsy of a collector raised to the highest power. Simulated black-and-white cowhide decorates chests of drawers and a cabinet, which holds a collection of cow creamers and assorted ceramic cows. Not surprisingly, a cow skin covers a side chair. Above, the old-fashioned bouquet of everyone's all-time favorite flowers—ranunculus, geraniums, lilacs, lisianthus, begonias, tulips, and lady's-mantle—sits sedately on a visual joke: the top of a discarded bureau painted to look like exquisite antique lace. In the believe-it-or-not category, all the furniture in this cow bedroom cost under $10, but of course this does not include the labor and love lavished on transforming these prize finds from junk to gems.

Opposite: *The canopy provides all the drama in this pared-down bedroom. A red-and-pink quilt adds a gentle eddy of color, as does the wingback chair. Local garden flowers—summer dahlias, astilbe, and snapdragons—are framed by the window molding left natural for a rustic effect.*

Above: *A white pitcher brimming with Queen-Anne's-lace, black-eyed Susans, thistle, and cornflowers looks naturally impromptu for this guest bedroom in a pine cabin in the Adirondacks. Red-and-white handmade quilts enliven the American four-poster pine beds.*

Below: *The bed and bedside table with a glass top show variations on the ever-popular willow theme, both created by Tim Barber. An English nickel silver lamp from a Cape Cod flea market illuminates another flea-market find, a print of a yellow perch. Nestled comfortably on the windowsill among an appealing collection of old paint boxes and bird dwellings is a cobalt blue vase filled with lupine, columbine, and wild flowers.*

Fresh flowers could be mistaken for trompe l'oeil in this most feminine of bedroom corners. A Victorian English ruby glass liner holds the radiant pink assemblage of miniature calla lilies, 'Angelique' tulips, sweet peas, 'Dainty Bess' roses, and lisianthus. The lace over pink silk-skirted dressing table is flanked by a silk damask French music chair and an elaborate gathered and poufed chintz balloon shade. A Queen Anne chinoiserie mirror reflects the delicate chinoiserie box surrounded by other elegant objects on the glass top. Nineteenth-century German engravings hang over a painting on porcelain, which is also nineteenth century.

Armfuls of perfect 'Champagne' roses, simply arranged in a nineteenth-century vase, presage the delicate floral themes of designer Charlotte Moss's bedroom. Her four-poster bed is covered in rose chintz;
a floral motif appears not only on the pillows but also on a delicately painted English washstand, on
prints and watercolors of botanical favorites, and on a charming little footstool paired with a French
baby chair. A Paris porcelain lamp illuminates an abundance of objects.

Biedermeier furnishings make particularly graceful floral counterparts. The pink and green silk-striped fabric on this Biedermeier chair seat suggested the delicate and delicately colored flowers—hybrid lilies, dahlias, scabiosa, lisianthus, 'Greta Garbo' roses, and 'Vivaldi' roses—as well as this frosted pink glass vase atop the Austrian Biedermeier writing desk.

Opposite: Two sweet little bouquets, reminiscent of Victorian nosegays, fill matching red crystal vases. Summer dahlias, wild campanula, hemlock, cornflowers, and assorted wild flowers provide the only other dash of real color in this pretty, pristine room.

Sunlight anoints twin bouquets of cosmos in similar, but not matching, goblet-shaped vases. The radiance and delicacy of the pink blossoms and piercingly green leaves can be enjoyed one more time in a mirrored storage cabinet that looks so much a part of the room that it belies its portability. A richly patterned Fortuny spread on the bed, designed by John Saladino, inspired the hues, patterns, and textures of the abundant grouping of pillows. A pair of simple columnar lamps with white parchment shades doubles for ambient lighting in the room by day and reading in bed at night.

Bunches and bunches of snow-on-the-mountain, anchored in a large glass bowl, tumble over and caress the pair of eighteenth-century chaises-longues. The beige hue of the velvet upholstery fabric, restated in a tall, folding screen behind, is offset by the dazzling white of the flowers. The cool hues of the vases and bowls on the Récamier bench, conveniently used as a table, set up a cool contrast to the earth-toned Tibetan wool carpet. The simple stainless-steel lamp gives a nice fillip of machined modernity.

An arched door frame, outlined in naturally pale wood, and a gracefully curving door invite one to enter—in the most seigneurial manner—a high-ceilinged, grandly scaled, luxurious New York bedroom. An abundance of French hybrid delphiniums generously fanning out from an understated black vase on the floor provides the perfect counterpoint to the splendid marble mantel, dating to the 1920s, and Queen Anne chair. Both the antique wall sconce and the richly patterned carpets provide ornate antidotes to the classical spareness of the room.

The Bathroom

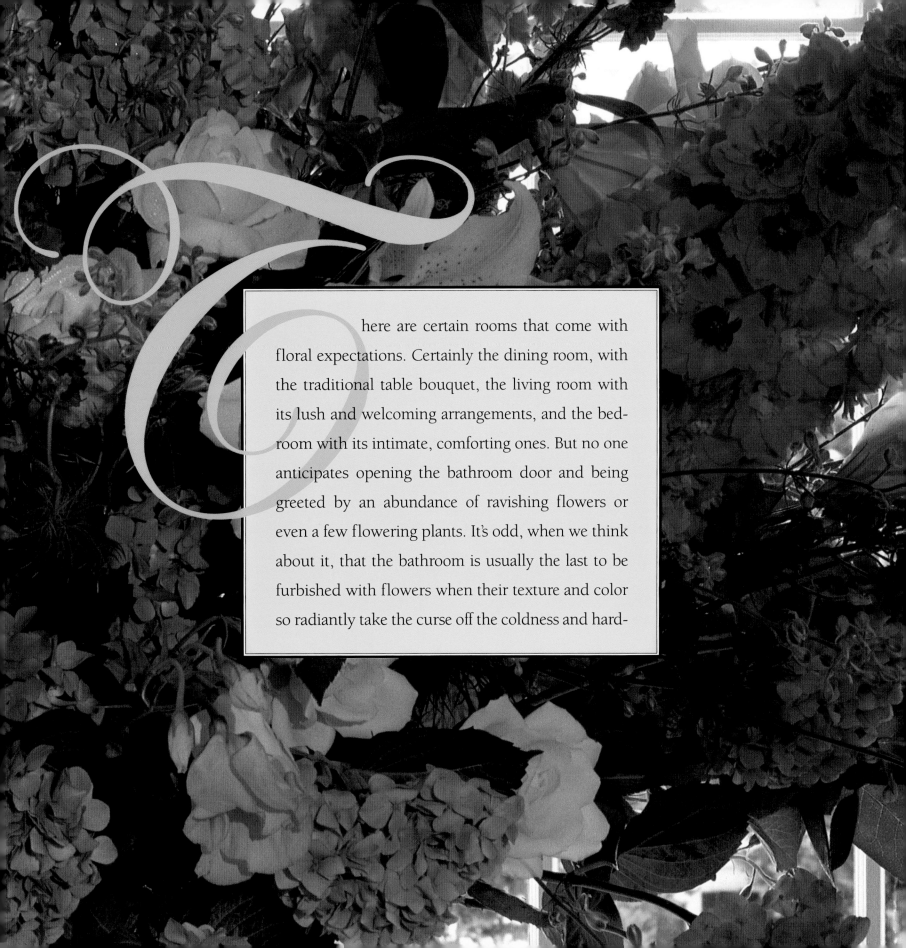

There are certain rooms that come with floral expectations. Certainly the dining room, with the traditional table bouquet, the living room with its lush and welcoming arrangements, and the bedroom with its intimate, comforting ones. But no one anticipates opening the bathroom door and being greeted by an abundance of ravishing flowers or even a few flowering plants. It's odd, when we think about it, that the bathroom is usually the last to be furbished with flowers when their texture and color so radiantly take the curse off the coldness and hardness of most of the surfaces there. While being undeniably pleasing decoratively, tile and porcelain are not the most comforting of materials.

The bathroom is the perfect place to display a flower container that doubles as an interesting decorative object. Permanently stationed there, it adds personality to a room that is often on the bland side. The fact that these objects were created for a purpose, not just as frivolous decoration, gives them a kind of integrity and functional beauty where every curve and furbelow counts.

Just as bathrooms benefit from flowers and plants, so the reverse is also true. The steamy warmth and humidity of the bathroom, particularly ones that hot shower devotees frequent, are as salutary for most flowering plants and cut flowers as a vacation on a tropical island is for us. Not surprisingly, the hothouse atmosphere of the bathroom actually prolongs the life of flowers and plants. Orchids achieve great success in the humidity. They respond to it as if they were wintering in a warm greenhouse. And what a delight they are when they start to bloom. There is something wonderfully sybaritic about walking into a bathroom and seeing a glorious orchid in flower—especially in a bathroom without a view of the outdoors. Though one would never expect it, austere little ivy does surprisingly well in the bathroom, too, especially if it has at least a modicum of light. For hardy northern souls who keep their bathrooms on the cool side, paper-whites are perfect. They not only bestow the gift of beauty but also that of fragrance. Surely one of the most delightful ways to relax is to stretch out for a long soak in the bathtub. If you close your eyes and inhale the heady sweetness, you'll imagine you're close to heaven.

Fragrance is a great plus in the bathroom. It does not overwhelm or surfeit because one usually spends much less time there than in other parts of the house. Scented flowers offer all the practical advantages of sweet-smelling soaps and perfumed bath oils plus the added bonus of being wonderful to look at.

One reason why bathrooms may seem incompatible with plants or flowers is that they are often small. But even in tight quarters, there's almost always a vacant spot on the back of the toilet where one can shoehorn a small plant or a few blossoms. The sink area could also accommodate a small vase. And a large edge at the back of the tub makes a fine setting for plants as well. Plants like amaryllis or paper-whites can go right on the floor. When there's a skylight, it makes sense to hang plants from the ceiling. Flowering jasmine is a delight hung this way.

For expressing your own personality in flower arrangements, the bathroom is a challenging and satisfying venue.

Wood-framed glass doors from an apothecary shop, vintage 1880, were refitted with mirror and installed in this tailored bathroom. A nineteenth-century American mirror, hanging above a Victorian marble-top walnut washstand, are a sympathetic match. A 1930s copper vase sports a casual arrangement of bright yellow ranunculus, without taking up too much space—a factor in most bathrooms.

An elegant French antique chair, more typically linked with the living room than the bath, becomes a decorative focal point against the sleekness of a curved marble counter top and vanity. A standing brass mirror and a blue Venetian vase pick up on the curves of the vanity. Cut jasmine in a water tube was chosen not only for its graceful beauty but also for its lovely scent, so appreciated in a bathroom.

Opposite: *The bathroom is the perfect spot for this tongue-in-cheek collection of Niagara artifacts: on the wall, a poster; on top of the toilet, pewter mats (tourist souvenirs from the 1930s) and vintage photos and postcards of the falls. An arrangement of Martha Washington geraniums, muscari, jasmine, sweet peas, and rambling roses lends vibrant color to a yellow flea-market vase, vintage 1940.*

Panels of boldly graphic black-and-white striped cotton canvas hang outside the bath like theater curtains. When pulled open, they frame a wooden flat of hot pink ranunculus with refreshingly cool green leaves. Just one dashing floral touch, like this, can add a needed bit of high drama to the functionally everyday.

Limiting the type of flowers to just one deftly echoes the understated spirit of this modern decor. Potted red begonias scattered about the floor of the bathroom, including a separate contingent in the shower stall and steam room, pep up the crisp black-and-white tiles and green marble. Subtle variety comes by way of the three different assemblages of blooms, joined with photos and fish, on the vanity. The red of a potted begonia sings out in a trio that includes subtle lady's-mantle and soon-to-bloom pink hyacinth.

An old-fashioned bathroom with its original 1930s hardware and frieze of blue-and-white shell tiles makes a charming setting for a casual little wild flower bouquet. Though understated, the floral variety, from the woodland around the house, is quite rich—fairy roses, loosestrife, mint, black-eyed Susans, and grasses.

What pure bliss! Imagine walking into this bathroom and seeing and smelling paper-whites, plus a bouquet of waxflowers, lisianthus, snow-on-the-mountain, dill, and cyclamen leaves in a pottery vase. The beauty of the wainscoted room with its porcelain sink and pink marble top adds to the pleasure.